Let's Talk About Going to the Dentist

Marianne Johnston

The Rosen Publishing Group's

New York

Published in 1997 by The Rosen Publishing Group, Inc.
29 East 21st Street, New York, NY 10010

First Edition

Book design: Erin McKenna

Photo credits: All photos by Seth Dinnerman.

Johnston, Marianne.
    Let's talk about going to the dentist / Marianne Johnston.
        p.   cm. — (The Let's talk library)
    Includes index.
    Summary: Describes what may happen during a checkup at the dentist's office.
    ISBN 0-8239-5034-4
    1. Dentistry—Juvenile literature. 2. Children—Preparation for dental care—Juvenile literature. [1. Dental care. 2. Dentistry.] I. Title. II. Series.
    RK63.J64 1996
    617.6—dc20
                                                    96-27193
                                                                 CIP
                                                                  AC

Manufactured in the United States of America

Table of Contents

Teeth Are Important

Lots of people hate brushing their teeth. But teeth need to be taken care of just like the rest of our bodies. Imagine what life would be like if you didn't have any teeth. You couldn't chew your food. You couldn't speak well. Did you know that your teeth help you speak clearly? It's hard to understand someone who doesn't have any teeth. If we don't take good care of our teeth, they get sick. They may even fall out. That's why we have to go to the **dentist** (DEN-tist). She helps us keep our teeth healthy.

◀ We need our teeth in order to eat crunchy foods like apples.

What Is a Dentist?

A dentist is a doctor who knows all about what's inside your mouth. The mouth is the only part of the body a dentist works on. He knows all about your teeth and if they are healthy or not.

If your teeth are healthy, the dentist just cleans them. If they aren't healthy, the dentist knows how to make them stronger. He can also show you how to take better care of them.

Dentists are specially trained to ▶
work on people's mouths.

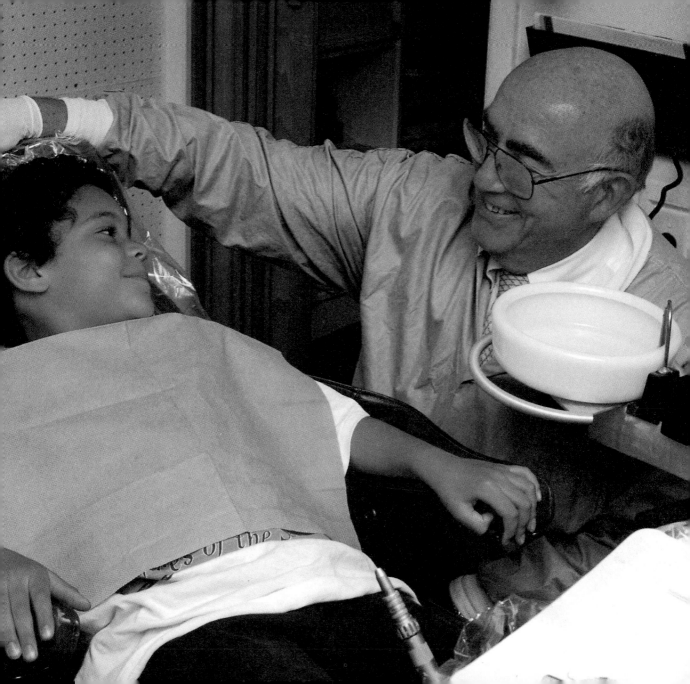

In the Waiting Room

When you first get to the dentist's office, you will have to wait in a waiting room. Your parents may have to fill out some forms. These will tell the dentist who you are and whether you've been to a dentist before.

Most waiting rooms have magazines or books to read while you wait. Some waiting rooms have toys to play with. But you may want to bring your favorite book or toy, just in case.

◀ If you're nervous while you're waiting, tell your mom. She'll explain what's going to happen when you see the dentist.

The Dentist's Helper

The first person you'll see when your name is called is the **dental hygienist** (DEN-tul hy-JEN-ist). This is the dentist's helper. She helps you into the dentist's chair. This is a big, comfortable chair. You can almost lie down in it. It also moves up and down. The hygienist hangs a paper napkin around your neck. This keeps the front of your shirt dry. Then the hygienist looks at your teeth. The hygienist is usually the first person to look at your teeth.

The hygienist makes sure you are comfortable before she looks at your teeth. ▶

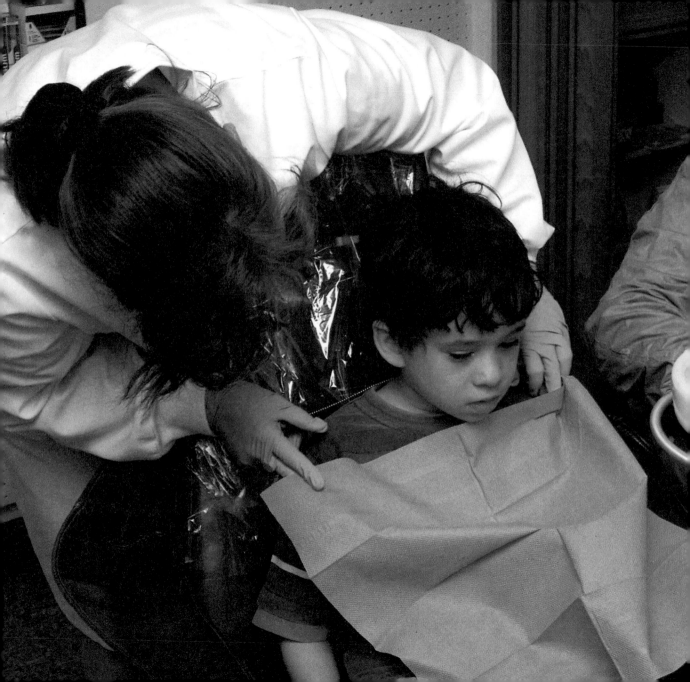

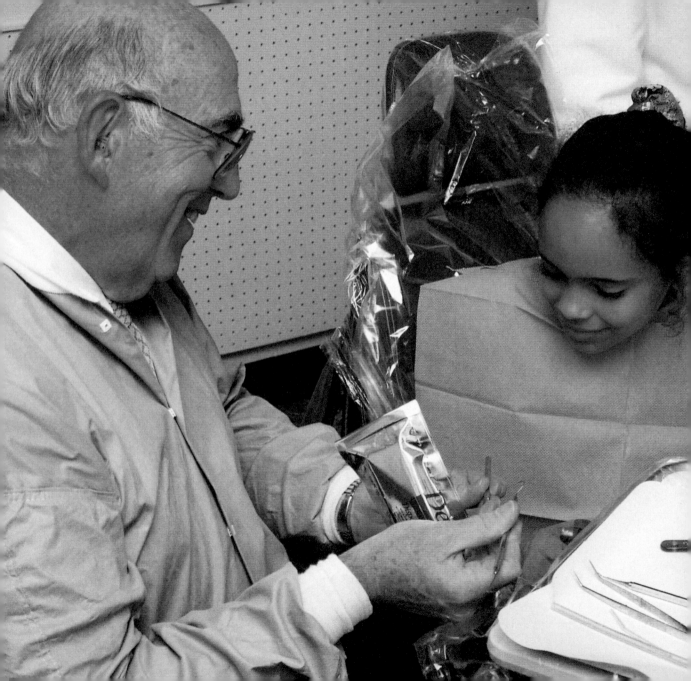

The Dentist

When the hygienist is finished, the dentist takes a look. He examines your teeth and gums to make sure they are healthy. Then the dentist, or sometimes the hygienist, gives your teeth a very good cleaning. Dentists use a special tool to clean your teeth. The tool has a smooth rubber tip that spins quickly. The spinning tip rubs away all the food and **plaque** (PLAK) from your teeth. It feels a little strange, but it doesn't hurt at all. Sometimes it tickles.

◄ Don't be afraid to ask the dentist to show you what his tools look like and how they work.

Special Tools

Dentists and hygienists use special tools to clean and check your teeth. An **explorer** (ex-PLOR-er) is a metal tool about the size of a pencil. It has a hook at the end. The dentist uses the hooked end to check your teeth. She also uses it to gently clean around the sides of your teeth. Dentists use a small rubber **suction** (SUK-shun) tube to suck the water and **saliva** (suh-LY-va) from your mouth. This makes your mouth dry, which feels funny. But it is easier for the dentist to work on dry teeth than on wet teeth.

You will probably see a tray ▶ with all of the dentist's tools.

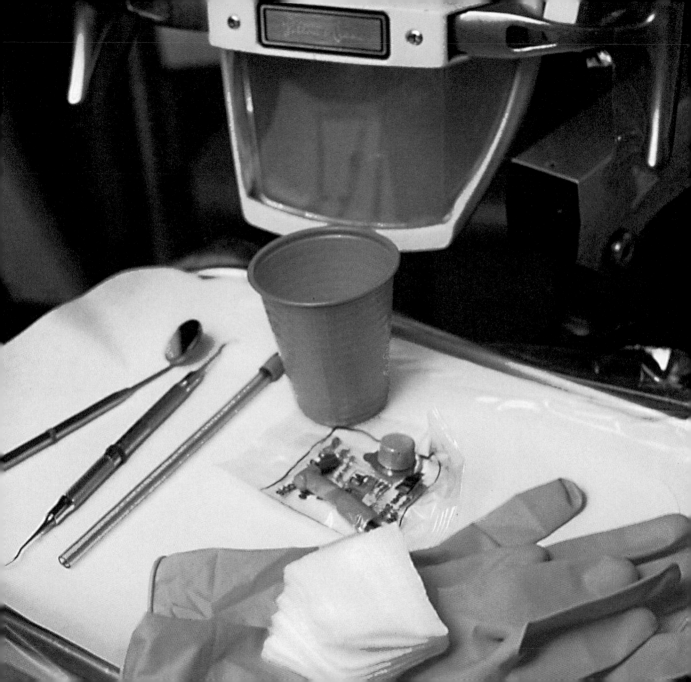

Cavities

When the dentist examines your teeth, he may find a **cavity** (CAA-vuh-tee). A cavity happens when a part of one of your teeth gets soft. The dentist must make the tooth strong again. He uses a drill to get rid of the soft part of the tooth. He fills that spot with a hard material called a filling. Then your tooth is as good as new. If the dentist thinks that the drilling will hurt you, he may give you a shot to **numb** (NUM) the area. The shot may pinch a little. But after that you won't feel anything until the dentist is finished.

◄ The dentist takes an X ray, or a picture, of your teeth to help him see if you have any cavities.

Braces

Sometimes teeth don't grow in the right way. If this happens, you may need **braces** (BRAY-sez). Braces are metal or plastic wires and bands. The dentist puts these on your teeth. The braces slowly move your teeth into the right place. You may have braces for a few years. They may hurt the inside of your mouth a little. You might have to avoid foods such as popcorn and gum because they get stuck in your braces. And you have to brush your teeth carefully. But when the braces come off, you will have a great smile filled with straight, healthy teeth.

Braces may feel funny for a while, ▶ but you will get used to them.

Advice from the Dentist

After your checkup, the dentist will tell you how to take good care of your teeth. You will learn how to brush your teeth properly and how to use **dental floss** (DEN-tul FLAWSS). Dental floss is a waxy thread that you gently slide between your teeth. It helps to get food and plaque from between your teeth. The dentist may tell you to eat foods that help your teeth stay healthy. Milk has **calcium** (CAL-see-um), which makes your teeth strong. Candy and sugary foods make your teeth weak. They may give you cavities.

◀ Foods with calcium, such as milk and cheese, are good for your teeth.

Time to Go Home

At the end of your visit, the dentist will probably give you a brand-new toothbrush. You may even be able to pick the color that you want. Some dentists give each child a toy to take home.

As you leave, your parents will set up your next checkup. Your checkups should be about every six months. Regular visits to the dentist keep your teeth strong and healthy and will give you a beautiful smile.

Glossary

braces (BRAY-sez) Metal or plastic wires and bands used to straighten crooked teeth.

calcium (CAL-see-um) Element that helps keep your teeth and bones strong.

cavity (CAA-vuh-tee) Hole or soft spot in a tooth.

dental floss (DEN-tul FLAWSS) Strong thread for cleaning between teeth.

dental hygienist (DEN-tul hy-JEN-ist) Dentist's helper.

dentist (DEN-tist) Doctor for teeth.

explorer (ex-PLOR-er) Tool used to check and clean teeth.

numb (NUM) Having no feeling.

plaque (PLAK) Thin covering of germs and food that forms on teeth.

saliva (suh-LY-va) Liquid in the mouth that keeps mouth moist and helps in chewing.

suction (SUK-shun) Taking liquid from an area by removing the air from that space.

Index